Aries
A collection of cosmic poetry

Denise Grace

Copyright © 2023 Denise Grace

All rights reserved.

Denise Grace

c/o COCENTER

Koppoldstr.1

86551 Aichach

ISBN: 979-8-3976-0839-8

DEDICATION

To my dear Aries friend,

This book is dedicated to the unstoppable spirit of the Aries, who fearlessly blazes trails and ignites the world with their boundless energy and unwavering determination. You are the pioneers, the trailblazers, and the catalysts of change. This book is dedicated to you. May these pages serve as a celebration of your vibrant existence, reminding you of the incredible power you possess to overcome any challenge and conquer new frontiers. Your courage inspires us all to embrace our own inner fire and pursue our dreams with relentless passion. To the Aries, the epitome of fearlessness and the spark that sets the world ablaze.

CONTENTS

INTRODUCTION   1

PERSONALITY   5

LOVE AND RELATIONSHIPS   93

LIFESTYLE   151

LIFE LESSONS   189

Dear Reader,

As you immerse yourself in the enchanting universe of this poetry collection, I invite you to embrace the diverse world of the zodiac sign Aries.

Yet, remember that the sun sign alone is just one facet of the complex constellation that is your birth chart. Your celestial identity is a symphony of various planetary influences, weaving a unique melody that resonates within you.

Not every poem may perfectly mirror your own experiences or fully capture the intricate layers that define you. And that is more than okay – it is beautiful. Embrace the delightful diversity within yourself and cherish the individual influences that shape your cosmic dance.

So let these poems ignite your imagination, inspire reflection, and celebrate the vibrant mosaic of your unique astrological identity. May you find resonance, amusement, and the sheer delight of discovering the vastness within you.

With cosmic wonders and infinite possibilities,
Denise

INTRODUCTION

Dear Aries,

You are the epitome of passion, determination, and unyielding spirit. Your fiery energy ignites the world around you, and your unwavering drive to achieve your goals is truly inspiring. Your courage knows no bounds, and you fearlessly venture into new territories, blazing trails for others to follow. Your enthusiasm is infectious, and it propels you to take on challenges with a passion that leaves a lasting impact on those around you.

Your independent nature is a testament to your inner strength and resilience. You possess a natural ability to lead, and your unwavering self-confidence inspires others. While your impulsiveness may lead you down unexpected paths, it is also a testament to your spontaneity and zest for life.

Remember, dear Aries, that your boldness and fearlessness have the power to ignite change and inspire others. Your determination and unwavering spirit are forces that can move mountains.

Sincerely,
Denise

Aries

Aries is the first astrological sign in the zodiac, symbolized by the Ram. It spans from March 21 to April 19 and is ruled by the planet Mars. Aries is a fire sign, characterized by enthusiasm, energy, and a pioneering spirit.

Aries, is a cardinal sign, initiating action and leading with fiery enthusiasm. They are like the spark that ignites new beginnings and ventures.

Those born under the sign of Aries are often seen as confident, assertive, and independent individuals. They are natural leaders who are not afraid to take risks and pursue their goals with passion and determination. Aries people are also known for their impulsiveness and can be prone to acting on impulse without fully thinking through the consequences.

Overall, Aries is considered a strong and dynamic sign, with a lot of energy and initiative. However, they can also be prone to impatience and a lack of tact.

PERSONALITY

Unleashing their fire, Aries takes the stage,
bold and confident, they never disengage.
With a spirit untamed and a heart that's true,
Aries, the trailblazers, daring and anew.

Their passion ignites, like a flame in the night,
driven and ambitious, they reach great height.
Independent souls, they march to their beat,
Aries, the pioneers, fearless and elite.

Direct and outspoken, they speak their mind,
opinionated and fierce, one of a kind.
Their loyalty runs deep, unwavering and strong,
Aries, the steadfast, where friendships belong.

In love, they're intense, a blazing desire,
romantic and devoted, they never tire.
Their love language bold, with sparks in the air,
Aries, the lovers, a passionate affair.

So let's celebrate Aries, the stars align,
with charisma and energy, they brightly shine.
Their vibrant personalities, a force to behold,
Aries, the warriors, with stories untold.

Aries

I am Aries.
I am the fiery leader, ablaze with boundless energy and vitality.
I am the embodiment of all or nothing,
driven by the grand vision, not bogged down by details.
I spread like wildfire, swift and unstoppable. The sound of a crackling fire and the invigorating scent of freshly cracked red pepper, symbolizing my fiery and energetic nature.
I am your ambition personified, leading with fervor and unwavering passion.
I am the instant when fear recedes into the shadows,
a moment of pure courage.
I am never the patient one but the fiery temperament you require.
I stand as the independent trailblazer, carving a path for you to follow with confidence.
I am the driving force in the room, the catalyst of action. The spark that ignites new beginnings and sweeps away the old.
I am the warrior who charges into battle, unafraid and undeterred. My impulsive nature is the source of my daring and my strength.
I am the embodiment of resilience, rising stronger with every challenge.
I am the pioneer, unafraid to walk alone and set the pace for others.
I am Aries, forever bold and unyielding.

Courage is Aries' middle name,
for they fearlessly dive into the unknown,
turning every challenge
into an opportunity to shine.

Aries

It's not that I've never felt fear;
I simply don't let it dictate my actions.

Denise Grace

On the German highway,
where speed has no say,
lighting cigarettes with a gaze,
in leather and boots we sway,
in the cinema,
laughter in a horror movie's array,
arm wrestling the bartender,
a challenge to display,
in a fearless community,
where words don't betray,
beneath the bright fire's display,
we find our way.

Aries

Born to lead,
destined to conquer.

What I love:

Clear-cut communication.
Efficiency and swift actions.
Taking the lead without coercion.
Engaging in high-energy physical activities.
Passionate and vibrant relationships.
Having things go my way.
Spontaneous adventures that ignite my spirit.
Parties and lively gatherings.
Embracing my inner child's spirit.
Confronting work challenges head-on.
Defending everything of importance to me.
Cherishing physical touch and quality time.
Taking bold risks.
The thrill of the chase and pursuit.
Flirting and playful banter.

Aries

When an Aries enters a room,
their confidence commands attention,
leaving no doubt about their presence.

Denise Grace

In a world of people pleasers,
they stand tall as the nonconformist,
prioritizing their own desires and aspirations,
unafraid to ruffle a few feathers along the way.

Aries

If you could fathom the anger I harbor within,
you'd comprehend why I release some;
there's no space left,
and it devours me from within.

No limits
when it comes to ambition,
the hunger for success is the fuel
that powers the unwavering
pursuit of greatness.

Aries

I don't wait for opportunities,
I create them.

The blunt response,
the energy drink,
the fast car,
the trained body,
the broken rules,
the loud laugh,
with the bright daylight just for you.

– the epitome of action

Aries

Fire in their spirit,
strength in their soul.

Denise Grace

Brushing off hurt with a smile,
but the sensitivity lingers,
reminding them of their capacity
to feel deeply.

Aries

In words sharp as blades, they speak,
direct and fearless, their truth they seek.
No sugar-coating, no beating around,
with honesty bold, their message profound.

Burning fire within me,
a rage as deep as hell,
impossible to be contained.
But the moment that hellfire
turns into a small flickering light,
remorse comes creeping up on me again.

Aries

The epitome of
strength and resilience.

A cardinal fire sign,
Aries ignites the zodiac with its fiery energy. They lead with passion and spontaneity, setting the pace for new beginnings. Aries is the spark of spring, breathing life into every adventure. Aries' bold, masculine, and assertive energy aligns with the archetype of a conventional leader.

Aries

Confidence is woven into
the very fabric of my being,
radiating from me
like a captivating aura.

Denise Grace

Telling them not to do it
only fuels their desire
for immediate action.

Aries

Words,
potent arrows in discourse,
deliver verbal punches with force,
leaving bruises,
a linguistic course.

The obsession is a constant companion.
It could be a favorite meal,
a newfound hobby,
a person, or the burning desire
to relocate to a foreign land once more.
It all can shift in an instant,
but in that very moment,
it feels undeniably real.

Aries

Speaking with a direct fire,
their straightforwardness,
their unique desire.

Growing up is overrated;
I prefer to dance through life
with a skip in my step
and a mischievous grin.

Aries

Unleashing passion
with every step.

Aries, ruled by Mars,
the planet of action, aggression, and primal passion,
emerges as the spirited commander of the zodiac,
fueled by an invigorating blend of determination and
dominance.

Aries

In the boundless theater of life,
courage takes the lead,
stepping boldly onto the stage,
ready for each brave deed.

Denise Grace

An opinion
for every occasion,
ready to share
without hesitation.

Aries:
the zodiac's living embodiment of
'Hold my drink, I've got this.'

Denise Grace

Staring in the mirror,
it often feels like life's a competition for me,
unable to simply relate to others.

Aries

Born with a warrior's heart,
unyielding from the start.
With every challenge, they rise higher,
fueled by a burning desire.

Fearless and fierce,
a force to be reckoned with.

Aries

"My way or the highway," they say with pride,
impatient hearts in life's fast stride.
Competition's fire, a flame burning bright,
never yielding, never out of fight.

With resolve akin to stone,
they stand resolute,
anchored to their convictions,
defying life's dispute.

Aries

Before I can rise anew,
all must crumble,
a phoenix's fate,
in ashes I'll be found.

Denise Grace

Ambition is the fuel
that powers my engine,
foot on the pedal,
no speed limit in sight.

Aries

Aries, guided by Mars's fiery light,
charges forth with unwavering might.

When an Aries says
'I'll be there in five minutes,'
they actually mean
'I'll be there when I'm done
conquering the world.'

Aries

I am the captain of my destiny,
charting my own course.

Headfirst into challenges, they go without pause,
opinionated, their voice a resounding applause.
Expressive as hell, emotions untamed,
in the arena of life, they're not to be tamed.

Aries

Life's pace is mine to set,
and I choose not to be slowed down.

Boldness is their trademark,
greatness their destiny.

Aries

In Aries' veins,
ambition fiercely thrives,
turning dreams to realities,
where life derives,
challenges become stepping stones,
it contrives,
in their quest for success,
their spirit survives.

Denise Grace

The eternal wellspring of youth
flows within the depths of my being,
coursing through the intricate network of my veins
like a revitalizing river,
bestowing upon me the timeless gift of vitality.

Aries

I'm the searing heat of passion's fire,
a wildfire's blaze, a summer's desire.
Burning asphalt in the scorching sun,
in winter's chill, I'm the warmth you've won.
Unconfined, I'm the good and the bad,
in every aspect of life, I'm the fire you've had.

Aries, the warriors of the zodiac,
fighting battles, never looking back,
with courage as their shield, they stand tall,
fearless in the face of any downfall.

Aries

The fire within me blazes,
I can't confine,
it burns, must escape,
else scar this heart of mine,
yet, when I see others scorched
by impulsive flight,
I yearn to rewind time,
make wrongs right.

Denise Grace

Presenting a bold and assertive exterior,
yet within, a kaleidoscope of emotions resides,
often unnoticed, eclipsed by my dynamic nature,
a depth of feelings, concealed behind the tides.

Aries

Waiting tests their limits,
that's for sure,
Aries' low patience
is hard to endure.

Stubbornness, a force within,
challenging adaptability, testing where to begin.
Yet in this struggle, strength does reside,
a balance struck as we navigate life's tide.

Aries

Living life on their own terms,
blazing their unique path.

Denise Grace

Sometimes, I feel as though I was born in the wrong era.
My true home is with nature, where I come alive.
Forging new paths through the wilderness.
When I'm out there, it's as if I've found my natural habitat.

Aries

Hidden beneath the fiery exterior,
Aries carries a sensitive heart
that few have the privilege to witness.
It's when this sensitivity is unseen
that sparks of anger can ignite.

Conformity?
Not in Aries' vocabulary.
They thrive on rebellion,
rewriting the rules as they go.

Aries

Your courage is a compass
that guides you through the storms,
leading you to calmer seas
where your dreams await.

Denise Grace

In the kingdom of immaturity,
I claim the throne,
Age is just a number,
in my playful zone.

Aries

Fueling life
with relentless determination.

Denise Grace

Fear may knock at their door,
courage swiftly replies,
doubt and hesitation,
in the face of greatness,
it defies.

Aries

The wild child, barefoot in the woods,
with the world as vast as it should,
the naughty one, no fear to bind,
challenges embraced, a free-spirited mind.

The rule breaker, ignoring the norm,
rolling eyes, tongues out, in any storm,
not a bad child, just unapologetically me,
a unique spirit dancing, forever wild and free.

Denise Grace

In the realm of passion, they ignite,
Aries, with their spark so bright.
A blazing flame, wild and free,
fueling dreams and destiny.

Unapologetically authentic,
fiercely original.

Denise Grace

For so long, the nice child I portrayed,
but within, anger silently swayed,
but it was you who unleashed this hidden part of me,
revealing the depths of emotions, I hadn't let free.

Aries

The trailblazer, ever bold,
in their hearts, adventures unfold,
with spirit untamed, they fear no fall,
leading in life, they conquer all.

Denise Grace

The masters of verbal sparring,
leaving opponents speechless and bruised...
in the ego.

Aries

Setbacks,
nothing but momentary shades,
my determination,
an eternal flame,
never fades.

Denise Grace

Without the brave,
we'd forever dwell,
in the known, the safe,
our own little shell,
for me personal,
my absolute hell.

Aries

The best in you,
the beauty in the pain,
the raw scream,
the resilience through storms,
the strength in the stumble,
the wisdom in the fumble,
the sunrise after the darkest night,
the flight when the world's too tight.

Denise Grace

Fearless leader,
wanderlust-filled
road trip,
90s straight jeans,
white t-shirt,
eternal sunshine,
embracing life's
simple pleasures,
moonlit beach party,
chocolatey warmth,
braided hair,
gleaming smile,
wild, untamed wilderness.

Aries

Defying limits,
rewriting the rules.

Denise Grace

Mars, the warrior in the sky,
with fiery spirit, he does fly.
A planet of passion and desire,
burning bright with celestial fire.

Aries

With a fiery spirit
that won't stand still,
Aries finds patience
a difficult skill.

Denise Grace

Aries, a burst of energy and might,
guided by passion, shining so bright.
In their journey, they never relent,
fueling dreams with an unwavering intent.

Aries

Their ambition is like
a never-ending game of 'Level Up.'
They're always aiming
for that high score in life!

They're the living embodiment
of 'act first, think later' philosophy.

Aries

Aries, fiery and bold,
with a spirit that can't be controlled.
Fearless warriors of the zodiac,
leading the way and never looking back.

Denise Grace

With a spark that never fades away,
Aries dances through life,
full of vibrant energy every day.

Aries

Headstrong like a charging ram,
Aries fearlessly follows their own plan.

Denise Grace

Your ambition is a force
that disrupts the ordinary
and births the extraordinary,
leaving an indelible mark
on the world.

Aries

Warn them not to proceed,
with that mischievous gleam,
Intrigued by the challenge,
it's part of their scheme.
They'll dive right in,
with a grin ear to ear,
Ignoring all caution,
letting go of their fear.
"Tell them not to do it,"
you earnestly say,
but they're drawn to the thrill,
in their own special way.

Mars,
the fiery guardian of ambition and drive,
ignites the spirit and fuels the journey
of endless possibilities.

Aries

Aries' sensitivity is a hidden strength,
adding layers of empathy and compassion
to their dynamic personality.

Denise Grace

The misfits who find strength
in their rebellious nature,
refusing to be confined
by society's expectations.

Aries

Courage is Aries' secret sauce –
they sprinkle it on their morning cereal
to ensure a fearless start to the day!

Denise Grace

Quick to flare,
their temper like a flame.
Handle with care,
or they'll never be the same.

Aries

My sadness runs as deep as the abyss,
expressed not in tears but in raw,
echoing screams.

LOVE AND RELATIONSHIPS

Aries in love

A relationship with an Aries is an exhilarating adventure of passion, spontaneity, and unwavering loyalty. They bring a vibrant energy and intense devotion to their partnerships. They approach love with an intensity that is hard to match. When an Aries falls in love, they dive in headfirst, embracing the exhilaration and the unknown.

Aries individuals are known for being bold and confident, and this extends to their romantic relationships. They are not afraid to pursue the one they desire and make their intentions clear. Aries individuals bring a sense of adventure to their relationships. They thrive on new experiences to keep the flame of passion alive. They are not afraid to take risks and push boundaries.

In a relationship, an Aries is fiercely loyal and protective. They will go to great lengths to defend and support their loved ones. Their passion extends beyond words and is expressed through their actions. They are willing to fight for their love and invest their time and energy. However, Aries can be independent and require their personal space. They value their freedom and individuality and appreciate a partner who understands and respects this need. Communication is key for an Aries in a relationship. They are direct in expressing their thoughts and feelings. They appreciate open and honest conversations.

An Aries in love is passionate, adventurous, and fiercely devoted. Their bold and direct nature make them an unforgettable partner for those who are ready to embrace their fiery spirit.

Aries in friendships

In friendships, an Aries is an enthusiastic and loyal companion. Aries individuals are natural leaders. They bring a contagious enthusiasm to their friendships, inspiring their friends to step out of their comfort zones. With their confident and dynamic personality, Aries tends to take the lead in planning outings and organizing gatherings. One of the defining traits of an Aries in friendship is their unwavering loyalty. They are fiercely protective of their friends and will stand up for them without hesitation. Aries is always there to offer support and advice.

Aries individuals are known for their direct and honest communication style. They appreciate open and straightforward conversations, and they expect the same from their friends. Aries values authenticity and dislikes drama. They will always speak their mind, even if it means having difficult conversations.

Aries is always up for an adventure. They love trying new things, exploring new places, and embarking on adventures with their friends. While Aries is known for their independence, they deeply appreciate and cherish their close friendships. They may have a large circle of acquaintances, but they have a select few who they truly open up to and consider as their inner circle.

In summary, an Aries in friendship is an energetic, loyal, and adventurous companion. They bring excitement and enthusiasm to the lives of their friends and are always ready to take the lead in creating unforgettable experiences.

Denise Grace

In love, the raging storm,
drenching their partner in torrents
of passionate affection and unwavering devotion.

Aries

The fooling around,
living every moment to the fullest,
the whirlwind passion,
spontaneous exciting dates,
the endless hugs and kisses,
the random calls during the day.
Did you hear my 'I love you'?

Denise Grace

In one unforgettable night with you,
I've collected wild stories that need no grandchildren to
recount. I forgot my fears in your whirlwind of courage,
sneaking into that sold-out concert, riding on the back of a
motorcycle with the wind painting our faces.

Aries

A crush,
red cheeks,
my playful side,
the exhilaration of flirtation
a potential love connection.
I'm all in.

I love like a child loves the movie
they want to see every second day,
like their favorite candy, their beloved toy,
they wouldn't share with anyone.
Like the endless weekend full of adventures.
Like the young soul, the way I don't think,
I will ever be an adult.

Aries

Make-up sex
like a volcanic eruption of love and desire,
leaving no doubts about the passion
connecting us.

Denise Grace

A genuine friend,
no secrets concealed,
they're all in or nothing,
their emotions revealed.

Aries

Melting into one,
not like sand at the beach,
more like waves moving forward.
Not like roots growing together,
more like fire burning through the forest.

You're not just my lover;
you're my partner in crime,
my confidant, and my eternal flame.

Aries

When you need a rock to lean upon,
turn to Aries, unwavering and strong.

Our connection is bound not by tears,
but by the myriad of all other emotions
that serve as the glue, sealing our bond.

Aries

When faced with a battle,
their fiery spark ignites,
fearlessly they confront challenges,
unwavering in their fights.

Denise Grace

In Aries' friendship, truth unveiled,
with candid words, their loyalty sailed.
No sugar-coating, no masks to wear,
just unfiltered honesty, forever fair.

Aries

In the tempest of my moods,
our bond holds fast,
weathering my anger, passion,
and my fervent blast.
In your unwavering presence,
I've found the key,
to unbox my tender side,
bold and free.

Denise Grace

In the crowd,
Aries shines bright,
but in the arms of a trusted few,
they find their guiding light.

Aries

A crush for them,
akin to wildfire's blaze,
burning with fervent desire,
to win affection's grace.

Denise Grace

In love like a wild storm,
electrifying the air with their passion
and leaving a lasting impact.
Though time may part our ways,
my name forever etched on your heart stays,
your first love, in memory's maze.

Aries

Not seeking strife,
but when it nears,
we'll finish it,
with no fears.
Choosing battles wisely,
we engage,
in the fight
for what's right,

Denise Grace

In the whirlwind of our friendship,
a storm of emotions brewed,
and before we knew it,
we were dancing in the rain of love,
soaking in each other's affections.

Aries

They say revenge
is a dish best served cold,
but for Aries,
it's a dish they'll make sure
is piping hot.

Breakups may be tough, but an Aries understands that the end of one chapter opens the door to new possibilities. They embrace the unknown with courage and resilience.

Aries

Breakups may shake an Aries momentarily,
but they refuse to let it define them.
They bounce back with resilience,
ready to embrace new beginnings.

Aries' biggest turn-on is someone
who can match their intensity,
like a spark meeting gasoline.
They love a passionate partner
who can ignite their flames.

Aries

Aries' biggest turn-off is a lukewarm attitude,
as if someone served them
a cup of decaffeinated coffee
instead of a shot of espresso.

Denise Grace

In their friendship,
laughter echoes through the air,
creating memories beyond compare.

Aries

Love's journey with them,
an adventure untamed,
a tale of passion and wild flames.

Aries' love, a tempestuous affair,
their hearts aflame, they dare to dare,
in love's adventure, they find their thrill,
unrestrained passion, an electric thrill.

Aries

What do I yearn for more:
to be loved as passionately wild as the untamed sea
or to discover my tranquility within the gentle shores
of your soul?

Denise Grace

My river of honesty flows deep,
but it's not meant for those
who can't swim in the currents of truth.

Aries

The allure of our attraction;
can a love as untamed as ours
ever hope to endure?

Denise Grace

When it comes to Aries' love language,
actions speak louder than words,
but a little bit of verbal appreciation
and admiration never hurt!

Aries

Aries' love language is like an action movie
with explosions and grand gestures.
Show them love with epic surprises
and adventurous romance!

Denise Grace

In matters of the heart,
loving fearlessly,
diving headfirst into passion
with an intensity
that sets their world ablaze.
Love isn't crafted for the faint-hearted.

Aries

I tried to love you as you needed,
but my feelings came out in bursts,
a torrent of emotion crashing against you.
My anger,
a shield against the fear of losing what we had.

Denise Grace

In the fiery aftermath of an argument's eruption,
they prove that love and passion endure,
a steadfast eruption.

Aries

In matters of love, Aries takes the lead,
with ardent affection, they plant the seed.
Their love burns fierce, like a wildfire's glow,
captivated hearts, with passion they sow.

Denise Grace

Every cell in my body burns for your touch,
yearning for your love, aching with desire,
our passion a wild, unquenchable fire.

Aries

Love metamorphoses me into an unwavering sentinel,
fiercely safeguarding and treasuring your heart
with steadfast fidelity.

Denise Grace

Any war against your happiness
is mine to fight.

Aries

A rollercoaster of passion, an adventure untamed,
with direct communication, our souls were inflamed.
You took my hand, no hesitation, it was done,
in that thrilling ride, I knew you were the one.

Denise Grace

Don't ponder my departure,
as my straightforward honesty
often collided with your sensitivity,
leaving me feeling like an elephant
in a porcelain shop.

Aries

Aries, a friend with boundless energy,
their enthusiasm and drive, a vibrant synergy.
With their adventurous spirit, they'll never tire,
in Aries' friendship, you'll always find fire.

Prolonged eye contact,
laughter that melted
the heart,
secret handshakes,
races to the
ice cream truck,
"I'll be your guide,"
spontaneous dance-offs,
cinematic kisses,
drowning in music,
dynamic heartbeats,
my joy.

Aries

Aries in love, a force untamed,
their passion burns, forever unclaimed.
With every beat, their heart ignites,
love's conquest, their eternal fights.

An Aries' dating profile would read:

"Calling all daredevils and thrill-seekers! Are you ready to keep up with this Aries fireball? Strap on your seatbelt because I'm about to take you on the wildest ride of your life. I live for excitement, spontaneity, and pushing boundaries. If you're up for skydiving into the unknown, exploring uncharted territories, and embarking on adrenaline-fueled adventures, then let's ignite a spark together. Warning: I come with a side of fiery passion and a contagious zest for life. Swipe right if you're ready to join forces and conquer the world, one epic date at a time!"

Aries

With innate leadership traits,
Aries shines,
in the friends' circle,
the one who unites,
all the time.

Denise Grace

Swift to judge,
simple to misconstrue,
yet to a select few,
my gentle side reveals itself
beneath the flames.

Aries

Aries, a friend, always up for a thrill,
their spontaneity and laughter, a constant thrill,
with their honest words and unwavering zest,
in Aries' friendship, you'll be eternally blessed.

Denise Grace

With an Aries by your side,
you can rest assured
that they will fight tooth and nail
to protect and support you.

Aries

Love unveils the gentle soul within them,
unveiling their profound well of tenderness
and their longing to envelop their beloved
in an embrace of affection.

My ideal partner,
a marathon runner's endurance they possess,
with the patience of a saint, a rare find, I must confess,
hunting for this unicorn, a quest, nonetheless!

Aries

A bull charging at a red flag,
ready to bulldoze through the argument
with their stubbornness.

Despite the fallen petals on the floor,
your growth towards me never ceased.

Aries

Love's adventure, Aries embarks,
with daring spirit, they make their mark.
In love's embrace, they find their might,
Aries love, a brilliant light.

LIFESTYLE

The perfect day

From the moment they open their eyes, Aries' perfect day is fueled by excitement and determination. They jump out of bed, ready to conquer the world with their fiery energy. They start their day with a vigorous workout, pushing their limits and setting the tone for the day ahead.

Afterwards, they indulge in a hearty breakfast, savoring each bite as they fuel their body and mind for the challenges to come. With their energy levels high, they dive into their tasks, tackling them with focus and enthusiasm.

Throughout the day, they seek out new adventures and experiences. Whether it's exploring unfamiliar places, engaging in thrilling activities, or taking on new projects, they embrace the unknown with open arms. In the company of friends, they shine even brighter. Their natural charisma and magnetic personality draw people in, and they effortlessly light up any gathering with their infectious energy and genuine enthusiasm.

As the day draws to a close, they reflect on their accomplishments and take a moment to recharge. They find solace in their own company, cherishing the quiet moments of self-reflection and rejuvenation. With a sense of contentment and fulfillment, they drift off to sleep, eagerly anticipating the adventures that await them.

Aries

The perfect holiday

Aries' perfect holiday would be an exhilarating and dynamic adventure, filled with excitement and exploration. They crave thrilling experiences and seek destinations that offer a blend of adventures and cultural activities.

They might choose to embark on an active vacation, indulging in activities like hiking, rock climbing, or water sports. The thrill of pushing their limits and conquering new challenges fuels their sense of adventure.

They also have a penchant for discovering new cultures and immersing themselves in local traditions. They would love to explore vibrant markets, taste exotic cuisines, and interact with the locals to truly understand the essence of the destination.

In their perfect holiday, there would be no shortage of opportunities for spontaneous adventures and unplanned detours. Aries thrives on the element of surprise and enjoys embracing the unknown.

While they appreciate moments of solitude and reflection, Aries' holiday is best enjoyed in the company of like-minded individuals who share their sense of adventure and zest for life. Whether it's friends, family, or a group of fellow adventurers, the energy and enthusiasm of their companions only amplify the joy of their holiday.

Ultimately, Aries' perfect holiday is one that leaves them with incredible memories, a sense of accomplishment, and a renewed passion for life.

The perfect work environment

In Aries' perfect work environment, the atmosphere is dynamic, fast-paced, and filled with opportunities for growth and achievement. They thrive in environments that allow them to take charge, make decisions, and showcase their leadership abilities.

Their ideal workplace is one that values their independent and innovative nature. They prefer having autonomy and the freedom to pursue their ideas and initiatives without excessive micromanagement. Aries excels when given the space to take risks and make bold moves.

Aries also appreciates a work environment that promotes healthy competition. They thrive when surrounded by ambitious colleagues who challenge and inspire them to push their limits. They enjoy a team that encourages and rewards their drive for success, creating a stimulating atmosphere where they can showcase their talents.

The perfect work environment for an Aries is one that fosters growth and offers constant opportunities for learning and advancement. They enjoy taking on new challenges and expanding their skills. Aries' ideal work environment recognizes and rewards their achievements. They appreciate acknowledgment for their hard work.

Overall, an Aries thrives in a work environment that embraces their ambitious and independent nature, encourages healthy competition, promotes growth, and recognizes their accomplishments. When provided with the right balance they are unstoppable.

Aries

Living life with passion, seizing opportunities, and leaving a trail of excitement in their wake.

Denise Grace

In the realm of leadership,
with a fire ablaze within,
a fervor to guide, inspire,
and make dreams begin.
Leading with passion,
through thick and through thin,
in moments of challenge,
I always dig in.
The flames of determination,
they burn bright and high,
a vision to follow,
a mission to fly.
Through hardships and trials,
I'll never be shy,
for the fire within me,
will never run dry.

Aries

Enter their abode,
embrace the vibrant vibe,
their energetic aura
warms every room inside.
With infectious zeal and zest,
life's joy they provide.

Denise Grace

As for routines,
they share a complex bond, you see,
spontaneity's their middle name,
where they'd rather be.
Impulses guide them more than schedules,
wild and free.

Aries

The thrill of adventure,
with heart racing free,
from mountains to oceans,
wherever it be.
Seeking the rush,
in each new leap,
embracing the wild,
that's the key to me.
Scaling the heights,
on cliffsides so steep,
with ropes and carabiners,
I dare to leap.
Surfing the waves,
where the ocean's deep,
in thrilling escapades,
my soul takes its keep.

Denise Grace

The rush of adrenaline surging through my veins,
from scaling mountains to skinny dipping in the sea,
rollercoaster rides and tasting the spiciest chilis,
all moments that truly make me feel alive.

Aries

In the rhythm of movement,
their spirit comes alive,
for every physical endeavor,
a piece of their soul they strive to revive.

Denise Grace

Living life like a kid in a candy store,
with a heart full of wonder, I explore.
Every day's a treat, a sweet surprise,
in this vacation, where joy never dies.
I skip down the street with a skip in my stride,
no worries, no stress, nowhere to hide.
My laughter is loud, my smile so wide,
in this candyland life, I always reside.

Aries

In the workplace:
Ambitious spirits,
driven hearts,
conquering challenges,
they play their parts.

Denise Grace

Home, their sanctuary,
blends comfort with delight,
in spaces that evoke joy,
day or night.
Cozy nooks for relaxation,
dynamic for social might.

Aries

In the arena of competition,
they don't just participate; they dominate,
turning every challenge into a chance to shine.

Denise Grace

In their lifestyle,
spontaneity's the norm they hail,
adventure's a daily must, patience?
A fairy tale.

Aries

Living life at full throttle,
Aries knows no boundaries or limitations.
Their lifestyle is a testament to their boundless energy
and fearless pursuit of what sets their soul on fire.

Denise Grace

On vacation,
their vibrant energy's
a constant friend,
infusing every moment with thrill,
no matter how it may bend.
Simple activities
transform into adventures,
to no end.

Aries

Balancing ambition
with a life's zest they choose,
a lifestyle,
purposeful and exhilarating,
they refuse to lose.

Denise Grace

In the mosaic of their existence,
every moment is an unplanned stroke,
every leap a daring dash,
and every endeavor an unwavering pursuit
of their dearest passions.

Aries

A natural leader, strong and bold,
in every realm, their story's told.
Guiding with grace, they light the way,
in work and life, come what may.

Denise Grace

In the grand theater of life, they star,
exploring every corner, both near and far.
From mountaintops to the depths of the sea,
they seize each moment, wild and free.

Aries

A dynamic workplace,
swift and unrestrained,
guiding all with my voice,
leadership unchained.

Denise Grace

I live life on my terms,
for a boss who dictates,
a new job awaits;
independence resonates.

Aries

When traveling,
Aries treads the path less known,
savoring authentic moments,
culture fully shown.
Creating lifelong memories,
seeds of adventure sown.

Denise Grace

From martial arts to rock climbing's lofty heights,
Aries thrives in hobbies that demand their might.
Strength, focus, growth – their passion takes flight.

Aries

Aries embraces life with unbridled zest,
their days painted with boldness, they manifest.
In action, excitement, they find their thrill,
alive in the moment, with a fiery will.

Denise Grace

In their careers,
Aries seeks roles with zest,
to shine as entrepreneurs,
be the very best,
thinking outside the box,
determined, they manifest.

Aries

In water,
on mountains,
or deep in a cave's embrace,
adventure I seek in every space,
an ever-moving chase.
New interests guide me
to my rightful place.

Denise Grace

Their lifestyle's a symphony,
passion's sweet vibration,
with determination,
they craft their own narration.
Marching to their drumbeat,
authentic desires in dedication.

Aries

Obstacles may loom,
but the destination's the guide,
always moving forward,
the course we'll adjust and ride.
In the darkest moments,
where hope seems to tear at the seams,
know that there's always a path
to reach our dreams.

Denise Grace

In the recipe of life,
I am the secret ingredient,
the spice that pulls it all together,
the unexpected twist,
the flavor that lingers,
making every moment unforgettable.

Aries

Leaving a mark on the world,
my highest quest,
screaming my name from mountain tops,
a life truly blessed.

Routine?
A foreign word to the heart of Aries,
they yearn for spontaneity's thrill,
the zest it carries,
ever ready to embrace life's unexpected strides,
with open arms,
they journey on the changing tides.

Aries

In work and life, rules they disdain,
for Aries, it's about breaking the chain.
They crave the freedom to chart their own way,
with passion and fire, they seize the day.

The playground of self-expression,
their cherished art,
through artistic,
musical,
or daring pursuits,
they impart.
Challenging societal norms,
they play their unique part.

Aries

In their professional,
Aries shines,
a powerful force,
merging passion,
strategic mind,
a determined course,
leaving a lasting mark,
they make success their source.

LIFE LESSONS

Let diplomacy be your ally,
Aries, as it fosters understanding,
bridges gaps, and paves the way
for harmonious relationships.

Aries

Listen attentively, Aries,
for in the art of listening
lies the wisdom of empathy,
connection, and deeper understanding.

Denise Grace

Flexibility is the key to growth, Aries.
By bending without breaking,
you can adapt to change
and embrace new opportunities.

Aries

Embrace the pause, savor the stillness,
for amidst the quiet moments,
the most profound revelations often unfold.

Collaboration fuels progress, Aries.
By working together,
you can combine strengths,
ideas, and talents
to achieve remarkable outcomes.

Aries

Reflection illuminates your path, Aries.
Take time to introspect,
learn from experiences,
and forge a deeper connection
with your true self.

Aries, you possess the power of emotional intelligence,
which enriches your relationships.
By comprehending and effectively communicating
emotions, you cultivate empathy, build trust,
and forge profound connections.

Aries

Seek balance in all aspects of life, Aries.
Balancing work and play,
ambition and self-care,
allows for a more fulfilling
and harmonious existence.

Denise Grace

Embrace and cherish your boundless energy,
for it's this fiery spirit that sets the world into motion,
igniting progress, and fueling the journey forward.

Aries

Long-term planning provides a roadmap to success.
Set goals, create a vision, and take steps
towards the future you aspire to.

Mindfulness anchors you in the present.
By savoring each moment, you cultivate gratitude,
awareness, and a deeper sense of inner peace.

ABOUT THE AUTHOR

As I embark on this literary journey, I, Denise Grace, welcome you into my world as a proud Libra and a passionate devotee of the mystical realm of astrology. Being a Libra myself, I have always felt a deep connection with the harmony-seeking nature of my zodiac sign. It is this intrinsic connection that ignited my curiosity and fascination with the celestial wonders that shape our lives.

From the moment I discovered the intricate art of astrology, it felt as though a veil had been lifted, revealing a universe of wisdom and insight. As a Libra, I found solace in the profound emphasis on balance, beauty, and meaningful connections that astrology offers.

Through the pages of this book series, I aim to share my love for astrology and its profound impact on our lives, all while keeping it light-hearted and playful. The intention is not to delve into the depths of complex astrological theories or make definitive predictions, but rather to celebrate the unique quirks and qualities of each zodiac sign.

Printed in Great Britain
by Amazon